eyes

on the

road

michell c. clark

THOUGHT
CATALOG
Books

THOUGHTCATALOG.COM

THOUGHT
CATALOG
Books

Published by Thought Catalog Books, an imprint of Thought Catalog, a digital magazine owned and operated by The Thought & Expression Co. Inc., an independent media organization founded in 2010 and based in the United States of America. For stocking inquiries, contact stockists@shopcatalog.com.

Produced by Chris Lavergne and Noelle Beams
Art direction and design by KJ Parish
Creative editorial direction by Brianna Wiest
Circulation management by Isidoros Karamitopoulos

thoughtcatalog.com | shopcatalog.com

First Edition, Limited Edition Pressing
Printed in the United States of America

ISBN 978-1-949759-76-1

For my wife and my daughter, who inspire me to be a better man, and subsequently a better writer.

To everyone who is searching for peace…

I hope that this book helps you to accept your past, embrace the present moment, and get excited about your future.

I hope this book helps you to keep your eyes on the road.

"Keep your eyes on the road."

I heard this phrase from my father, right before I sat in the driver's seat of our family's green Ford pickup truck for the first time. I was fifteen and a half years old. He gave me one of the loving but firm looks that fathers give their firstborn sons, and then we were off. He drove us down the road to the nearest high school, so that I could safely swerve all over the empty parking lot next to the tennis courts.

"Keep your eyes on the road."

Neglecting his instructions wasn't consequential—not yet. Then, a few weekends later, I left the safety of the parking lot. I turned left onto a busy two-lane boulevard, checking my rearview and side mirrors obsessively to make sure that I was staying in my lane—because now, one small lapse in focus could have me swerving directly into oncoming traffic, or into a grassy ditch. One second of compromised focus could lead to huge consequences.

I got in three car crashes before I graduated high school. Two of them were my fault. My teenage mind was no match for the distractions that came with being a high schooler with friends, a car, a cell phone, and a decent sound system. None of the tasks required for safe driving were complicated—it was a matter of staying focused on the fundamentals, no matter how many urges popped into my head.

"Keep your eyes on the road."

Today, this phrase is permanently engraved in my subconscious. I still get distracted, but I can't afford to stray off course. If I got in a car crash today, I wouldn't call my parents—I'd call my insurance provider. I might have my wife next to me. My daughter might be in the backseat. If my car was totaled, there wouldn't be a school bus or a disgruntled parental figure ready to take me everywhere I need to go.

The stakes are higher.

So it goes with learning to drive, and so it goes with life. If high school is a parking lot, adulthood is a busy highway—we no longer have the luxury of idling in traffic. Some of us have specific destinations in mind. Some of us just know that we can't afford to sit still. We're all conditioned to remain in motion. None of us can control everything that we experience along the way.

This persistent feeling of urgency that we contend with keeps us moving, but at a cost—there's no time for introspection when rest stops are so heavily stigmatized. So, we keep moving. We weave through traffic, swerve around potholes, and cut off anybody foolish enough to get in our way.

We know that our pace isn't sustainable, but we

continue to press forward with the blind assumption that things will even out at some point in the future—but that future never comes, and as the road stretches on indefinitely, our eyes inevitably wander.

"Keep your eyes on the road."

I know that I should focus on what's in front of me, but my heart can never escape the gravitational pull of my rearview mirror. When I do manage to look forward, I see too much. On a good day, I'm overwhelmed with excitement about what the future could bring. I see a better life for me and my family. I see happiness and fulfillment. I see deep-rooted peace.

Other days, I feel paralyzed by the thought of how many obstacles are in front of me. I struggle to see a future where I don't make the same mistakes that held me back during previous chapters of my life. I'm burdened by intrusive thoughts that tell me that my life might not ever get any better. I see emptiness, and I wonder if anything of substance will ever fill all of that empty space.

I don't always "trust the process." I don't always enjoy my journey. Some days, I wonder if my self-trust is misplaced. Sometimes, intrusive thoughts push me into a space where I'm so scared of getting lost that I forget where I'm trying to go. For as long as I can remember, there's been a voice in my head—a voice that tells me that my greatest accomplishments were lucky breaks. This same voice tells me that my failures are tied to deficiencies that I can't fix—that I'm not good enough, and that I never will be.

During certain seasons of my life, I've given this voice too much power—but today, there's a new voice in my head. The more I learn to trust it, the louder it becomes. I do my best to listen to this voice, even when my insecurities are pulling me in a different direction. This voice reminds me that failure is inevitable, contrary to what my ego wants me to believe. It tells me the truth: that I've always been good enough, and that my low moments don't refute this truth. When I hit rock bottom, this voice reminds me to take a deep breath, be proud of myself for trying, and give myself the time that I need to get back on my feet.

This voice has always been inside of me, but as I've grown more aware of its existence, I've chosen to listen to it, nurture it, and—perhaps most importantly—believe it. Considering that the average human being has more than 6,000 thoughts per day, this is one of the most important choices that I make every day.

Some thoughts are fleeting—if left to their own devices, they vanish in the blink of an eye. Some thoughts are irrepressible—you can't ignore them, no matter how hard you try. Some thoughts are shifty—just when you think they're out of your head, they sneak back into the picture.

It's impossible to hone in on the thousands of thoughts that flow through our minds on a daily basis—instead, we experience reality subjectively, through the lens of our judgments, interpretations, and belief systems. We are beautifully imperfect human beings, and contrary to what we may believe, we don't process information rationally—we are subconsciously influenced by our cognitive biases—or in other words, the mistakes that our brains make while trying to simplify the complex world that we live in.

With this understanding, it's important that we ask ourselves: how are our belief systems impacting the way that we experience the world?

What voices are we listening to, and how are they influencing our thoughts?

A lot of us struggle to keep our eyes on the road ahead because of the voices of fear that we've been nurturing—and as we nurture these voices that chip away at our confidence, amplify our insecurities, and poke holes in our worthiness, we start to find more things to be afraid of.

Our brains become wired to look for threats before seeking out opportunities. We give away our power and agency in exchange for fear and defensiveness. Instead of seeing a future full of opportunities, we see a future in which we're doomed to repeat our past mistakes.

It's human nature to feel a broad spectrum of emotions, but ruminating over negative feelings without working our way out of them can be dangerous. A lot of the content that we consume contributes to the feelings of fear and inadequacy that we carry in silence.

We need to be intentional about giving ourselves the tools that we need to counteract these tendencies. I hope that this book helps. I hope that the affirmations and encouraging sentiments in the pages that follow give you more of the perspective that you need to build an inner dialogue rooted in self-acceptance, self-belief, and self-love.

I hope that this book helps you to re-discover a version of yourself that can more readily choose self-belief, reject excessive self-criticism, and opt into a more empowered mindset—so that the next time you feel like you're hitting rock bottom, you know that you won't be there forever. I hope that this book helps you to make peace with your past, embrace the present moment, and get excited about your future.

I hope this book helps you to keep your eyes on the road.

**Great things take time.
(It's you. You're the
great thing.)**

You had assumed that it would be safe to run from your inconvenient thoughts until you were ready to confront them, but you never felt ready to rock the boat, and you never ran out of convenient distractions to chase after, until your legs gave out.

You were hoping to orchestrate your own gentle awakening—but life punched you in the chest instead.

You never knew that clarity could sting until it did. You never knew that self-awareness could feel so incapacitating. You thought your revelatory moment would feel triumphant, but instead it knocked you off your feet. Now you're on your back, gasping for air, trying to figure out how you didn't see the punch that leveled you.

As you catch your breath and your eyes flutter back open, every inconvenient thought that you had been avoiding floods back into your consciousness. Your heart pounds through your chest as you come to terms with the fact that the life you're living isn't the life that you want. You remember all of the choice points along the way where you chose comfort and complacency over purpose and progression. You see how you've compromised who you are and what you stand for.

You look up and see your regrets standing over you, staring back down at you.

But as you lay there, exhausted from running in circles and dizzy from the impact of your head slamming onto the pavement, you manage to find the silver lining.

You realize that the same pain that shocks and stings has also awakened you to the new possibilities that you deserve. You know that you're not done fighting. You know that you'll get back on your feet. You know that you don't have to run anymore.

How do you pick yourself back up again?

Confidently. Deliberately. Decisively. Without shame. You forgive yourself in full. You believe in your ability to break the cycles that used to hold you hostage. You remember that your mistakes will never define you.

Sometimes I wish that my life was like a '90s sitcom.

I wish that every conflict would magically resolve itself after ten minutes of dialogue and a few commercial breaks. I wish that I only had to worry about making the basketball team, winning the fight after school, and asking my crush to go to prom with me.

I wish that life felt simple. I wish that I would be faced with enough roadblocks to feel accomplished, but never to the point that I would have to reckon with overwhelm or anxiety. I wish that I could always see the light at the end of the tunnel. I wish that there was a time limit for struggle.

I have yet to experience a season of life that offers me the predictability or simplicity that is an inherent element of a 30-minute television episode.

We are all living lives that extend beyond the margins of what any screenwriter could fit into a full season. Our experiences can't be condensed into a palatable storyline.

Many of us are left to carry burdens that are heavier than anticipated, for longer than expected—and some days, we wonder if we'll end up caving under the pressure.

We listen to well-intentioned but empty phrases like "things will get better" and "keep the faith" from onlookers who haven't felt the heat of the fires that we're walking through. Their positive intent doesn't negate the effects, as we're left feeling unseen, unheard, and unsupported.

When left unchecked, our prolonged feelings of frustration, inadequacy, and sadness have the potential to grow deeper roots, threatening our faith and stifling our imagination. We discard the dreams that used to inspire us, exchanging them for a sense of pessimism that we hope will protect us but instead only takes away from the joy that we could be experiencing in the present moment.

We don't consciously decide to give up hope, but without the right tools and mindset, society threatens to take it away from us. It's not your fault that you're feeling hopeless or inadequate, but you do owe it to yourself to be mindful of how you respond when negative feelings persist.

You've already worked so hard to get this far. You deserve to see the fruits of your labor. You deserve to experience the better days that are coming, even if you have to wait longer than you want for them to arrive. You deserve that deep, healing sigh of relief that only comes after the clouds roll away and the sun comes back out.

You've worked too hard to let a season of darkness convince you that there's no light at the end of the tunnel.

You haven't lost your magic. You haven't lost your drive. You haven't lost your talent. You can still climb mountains. You can still create something out of nothing. You just need to remind yourself what you're capable of.

Affirm:

My dream is worth fighting for. God gave me this vision for a good reason. I will use every tool at my disposal to see it through.

This world can be exhausting and traumatizing, but you deserve better. You deserve joy. You deserve ease. You deserve to be loved in the languages that resonate with your heart—and that starts with the way that you love yourself.

You will never hear another person's voice more than you hear your own. When you commit to accepting every part of yourself, decide that you are worthy of being loved, and choose to nurture your well-being, you create the foundation for a healthy and happy life.

The way that you love yourself doesn't have to look like the viral self-care videos dominating your social media feeds. The way that you pour into yourself doesn't have to impress other people. The way that you show up for yourself doesn't have to be newsworthy.

We can all love ourselves differently, based on who we are as individual people. I'm not talking about the easily digestible, aesthetically pleasing version of self-love. I'm not talking about living beyond your means, ignoring all forms of criticism, or running away from your problems.

I'm talking about choosing the type of self-love that pushes you outside of your comfort zone so that you can move towards a life that brings you true fulfillment. I'm talking about the type of self-love that pulls you towards self-actualization and deep-rooted joy. I'm talking about the type of self-love that fills you up and allows you to show up for the people you love without living in a long term, never-ending relationship with exhaustion.

Sometimes self-love shows up as a willingness to let dying connections fade away without a fight. It's natural for people to grow apart. You have no obligation to offer people continuity for continuity's sake.

It's a beautiful day to congratulate yourself for how far you've come and to remind yourself that the life you've been dreaming about is possible. It's a beautiful day to remember that gratitude and ambition can coexist. It's a beautiful day to remember that you're in control. It's a beautiful day to remember that you don't have to leave things up to chance.

It's you.

It's always been you.

You've always been enough, and it's not your fault that it took you so long to understand that, because this world can make us all feel unworthy—but there's a better life waiting for you on the other side of your commitment to fully embracing this truth.

When you understand that you're enough, you free yourself from deficit-based thinking and make space for healthy growth.

When you understand that you're enough, you empower yourself to choose happiness over conformity.

When you understand that you're enough, you give yourself permission to be proud of who you are right now instead of always feeling like you're one step away.

You don't have to
wait until January 1st
to change your life.

There is no "one size fits all" secret to success, happiness, or fulfillment. Life is less of a science, and more of an art—and beauty is in the eye of the beholder.

They were wrong for invalidating your feelings. They were wrong for minimizing your trauma. They were wrong for trying to tell you that you were overreacting, when you were simply telling your side of the story.

The people who try to gaslight you into feeling like your pain isn't real are not your people. Their lack of empathy cannot overrule the significance of your lived experiences.

You don't have to prove the validity of your experiences. Anybody who tries to put you on trial for speaking your truth doesn't deserve your trust.

Honor your healing process by acknowledging every emotion that courses through your veins.

You're better than the narrative that your anxiety is creating in your head.

You're more powerful than your fear would lead you to believe.

You're not defined by your lowest moments or the hurtful things that people say about you.

You get to define yourself, for yourself.

Please try to celebrate yourself as often as you critique yourself. You don't need the "tough love" that this world forced on you, you need to heal from it. You can choose soft love. You can choose gentle love. You can be kind to yourself while holding yourself accountable.

Sometimes, you need somebody to grab both of your hands, look you deeply in the eyes, and remind you that you're worth the investment—not because you're perfect, or because you've fulfilled your potential, but because of who you are.

You need somebody who will pull you close and wipe the tears off of your cheeks. Somebody who will allow you to unravel without judgment. Somebody you can trust with all of your self-defeating thoughts and inconvenient truths.

You need somebody who knows what you're capable of. You need somebody who will love the version of you that is fighting to survive just as deeply as they love the version of you that is ready to conquer the world.

You need somebody to squeeze you tightly and remind you of how far you've already come. You need somebody who understands how hard you fought to get here.

You need somebody to remind you that this isn't your first seemingly insurmountable obstacle. Somebody to remind you that you've always found a way.

You need somebody to remind you that self-belief is a choice, and that you don't need anybody else's cosign to bet on yourself. You need somebody to remind you that you're more powerful than your fear would lead you to believe.

And sometimes, on those days when nobody is around to dry your tears or hug you tightly, that somebody has to be you.

Shout out to everybody who has decided that the trauma they've inherited is not the trauma that they will pass on.

Affirm:

I love every part of myself. I'm
proud of the person that I'm
growing into. I have made peace
with every past version of myself.
I accept myself, in full.

Self-love shows up as a conscious decision to take up space when people would rather see you shrink yourself to accommodate their insecurities.

Self-love shows up as a willingness to distance yourself from anyone who repeatedly violates your boundaries, devalues your worth, or disrespects your passions.

Self-love is the shield that protects you from the negative projections of people who have yet to choose healing for themselves.

Self-love is the voice that encourages you to stop settling for scraps, because you deserve abundance.

Self-love is not about being selfish—it's rooted in the understanding that when you take care of yourself, you can show up as a healthier version of yourself, and that if we all show up as healthier versions of ourselves, the world is a better place.

You deserve a life that is rooted in something deeper than survival. You deserve to thrive. You deserve a life that fulfills you—but we don't live in a world that automatically gives us everything that we deserve.

Are you ready to go after the life that you really want? It's not an easy path, but it's worthwhile.

You'll have to set goals that pull you away from the path that has been conveniently placed in front of you, and towards your purpose. You'll have to separate yourself from opportunities that look good, but don't feel good. You'll have to tune out the noise and cultivate a level of clarity that allows you to hear, acknowledge, and honor your heart's desires.

You'll have to bet on yourself, again and again—even when the odds are against you. You'll need to dig deep into your subconscious and excavate a level of resolve that is more powerful than your fear of failure.

Sometimes growth looks
like letting go of beliefs
that have always felt
comfortable but have
never served you.

It's a beautiful day to choose yourself.

It's a beautiful day to recommit to the habits that bring you focus, clarity, and peace.

It's a beautiful day to stop dwelling on things you can't control.

It's a beautiful day to congratulate yourself on how far you've come.

It's a beautiful day to go after the life you really want.

"Never quit" sounds great—but sometimes you have to quit. Be willing to say, "this isn't what I thought it was," or "this doesn't appeal to me anymore." Remember that you can quit "the thing" without quitting on yourself. Remember that persistence and fluidity can coexist.

Sending love to everybody who is recovering from the sting of rejection. Sending love to everybody who is struggling to rediscover their confidence. Sending love to everybody who is trying to bounce back.

Affirm:

I'm in the right place at the right time. This is where I'm supposed to be. I'm ready to receive all the blessings that are waiting for me.

It's tempting to be ashamed of past versions of yourself—for the mistakes you made, and the things you didn't know.

If you wanted to, you could live in the past forever.

You could walk yourself through all of the conversations in which you should have spoken up for yourself.

You could play back the times when you should have gone after what you really wanted instead of playing it safe.

You could think about what might have happened had you not been so quick to quit on yourself.

You could beat yourself up over your past mistakes for the rest of your life—but when would you have time to live your life?

What would you gain from choosing to be imprisoned by your past when you could be building a future that facilitates your healing?

Sending love to everyone who feels like the black sheep of their family. Sending love to everyone carrying the weight of trauma that existed before they were even born. Sending love to everyone who struggles to accept themselves because it never felt like anybody else ever did.

Affirm:

I deserve all of the good things that are happening in my life. Instead of questioning my worthiness, I will make the most of every blessing and opportunity that God sends my way.

You've worked too
hard to let a season of
darkness convince you
that there's no light at
the end of the tunnel.

Do you see yourself, right now?

At this very moment—are you aware that you are a miracle?

Can you count all the ways that your existence, not to mention your success, is worth celebrating?

Yes, there's more to accomplish. Yes, there's room for improvement. And maybe you're not as far along as you want to be in life—but I hope you take time to give yourself credit for the fact that you're on your way.

You're making it. You're figuring things out as you go—and you don't always find the perfect solution, but you do always find a way. You push through fear, anxiety, and discomfort. Yes, you make mistakes—but you learn from them.

Life isn't always easy, or fun, or glamorous. When you're focused on specific outcomes, it doesn't always feel like things are lining up the way that they should—but when you zoom out and look at the big picture, gratitude is easier to find.

Being told "no" isn't the end of the road, it's a choice point: will you pivot, or will you persist?

You ever feel like you're the last item on your own to-do list?

There's never enough time in the day. By the time we finish doing what we have to do, self-care feels like an afterthought.

If something threatens our lives or our livelihood, we're quick to drop everything so that we can protect ourselves—because there is no deadline, responsibility, or obligation more important than our own survival.

That being said, our definition of survival should not be limited to our physical well-being—we should also be attaching urgency to the preservation of our mental health and emotional well-being.

Being alive is a blessing—and for as long as we live, we should think of life as a gift to be slowly unwrapped and enjoyed rather than an endless checklist to be managed.

Life is short—and if we're not careful, we'll spend so much time doing everything we "have" to do that we'll run out of time for things that we want to do. Please, make space for yourself. Please, make space for joy. Please, make space for the experiences that make you light up inside.

Make space to live your
life—not just survive.
It's never convenient,
but it's always worth it.

Stop assuming that solitude has to be lonely and start looking at it as an opportunity to understand who you are when there's no one left to perform for.

If the breakthrough that you've been working toward fell into your lap, it wouldn't be a breakthrough—it would be another small step forward that you could take for granted today and forget about tomorrow.

The breakthrough that you're working toward will be gratifying because of how hard you've had to fight for it. The breakthrough that you're working toward will be transformative because of the ways it's pushing you to grow into the version of yourself that can create it.

The breakthrough that you're working toward will be unforgettable because it will represent the moment in time when you proved to yourself that you could bring your thoughts to life.

**You work too hard to
let fear of rejection be
the reason you don't
get what you want.**

Self-love isn't always this fluffy, soft, flowy way of living.

Sometimes self-love shows up as the voice in your head that says "now you know got damn well…."

Speaking up for yourself can feel terrifying when life has led you to believe that you are responsible for managing other peoples' emotions rather than making space for your own.

Reclaim your power by prioritizing your truth over their ego.

Affirm:

I am powerful. My thoughts shape my reality. My habits can change my life. My ideas can change the world.

Forgive yourself for every time you thought about quitting on yourself.

Forgive yourself for every time you led with fear, instead of faith.

Forgive yourself for every time when you let your anxiety win.

Forgive yourself for every time when you lost control.

You're one well-executed
great idea away from
changing your life forever.

Just one.

A gentle reminder:

You can't pour from an empty cup.

Please, don't let your empathy for others
drain you to the point that you can
no longer show up for yourself.

Affirm:

I am proud of the person I am becoming. I am excited about what the future holds. I see growth in every area of my life. Every step forward is significant. Every victory is worth celebrating.

Sometimes it really is as simple as asking for what you want.

There are people in your life who love you deeply and want to show up for you, and they're patiently waiting for you to tell them what that can look like.

They care about you—but they're not mind readers. No matter how much they love you, they can't hear the things that you're not saying. They can't respond to your unspoken wants, needs, or desires.

I hope that you understand that you're worth speaking up for, and there's nobody better positioned to do so than you.

Say it with me:

"I want to make space for everything
I deserve, so I'm letting go of
everything that's in the way."

It's scary because it's unfamiliar, not because you're incapable.

Consider this a gentle reminder that we are all beautifully flawed humans, doing the best we can with what we have. Consider this a gentle reminder that the inevitable moments when we fall short do not define us. Consider this a gentle reminder that the learning never stops.

Pay attention to the way that you talk to yourself when you make a mistake.

Whose voice do you hear in your head?

Do you encourage yourself like a dear friend, or berate yourself like a cruel authority figure?

Do you know that you can do better next time, or do you assume that you'll never be good enough?

Do you love yourself during your low moments, too?

Be kind to the childhood version of yourself that didn't know any better.

Be kind to the present-day version of yourself that is struggling to break harmful and deeply embedded habits now that they do know better.

Be kind to the future version of yourself by committing to the habits that will move you closer to the life that you want for yourself.

Affirm:

I deserve a life rooted in love, peace, and fulfillment. I will separate myself from people, places, and situations that interfere with the life that I deserve.

It's true. Unfortunately, a lot of people won't celebrate you until your wins feel "big" enough to them—but you can celebrate yourself now. You can be proud of every step you take and every sacrifice you make. And you won't need other people's applause to be proud of how far you've come and how much you've grown.

Invest in relationships that don't require that you shrink yourself in order to feel accepted.

Negativity is contagious—but so is optimism.
Unhappiness is contagious—but so is joy.
Fear is contagious—but so is love.

If you feel like you're stuck in a never-ending cycle of self-doubt and self-defeat, I want you to know that you deserve better. You deserve a happy life. You deserve a peaceful life. You deserve to live a life that fulfills you.

Every day that you wake up presents you with another opportunity to build the life that you deserve. It won't fall into your lap—but you can create it, once you understand that this process starts inside of you.

You can start by understanding that while it's impossible to eliminate counter-productive thoughts, it is possible to be aware of them, and to manage their impact. Acknowledge and push back against negative thought patterns when you realize that they're re-emerging.

When your mind tells you that "everything is going wrong and nothing matters," ask yourself if that's a thought rooted in truth or rooted in fear.

When your mind tells you that "nobody cares about you," remind yourself that losing touch with people doesn't mean that they've stopped loving you.

When your mind tells you that you're not good enough to accomplish the task at hand, think about all the times you exceeded your own expectations.

Take a break when you need to, instead of waiting until you think you "deserve" one. Rest is not earned, it's required.

It's never too late to reconnect with your passions.

It's never too late to recommit to the dreams you gave up on.

It's never too late to become the person you were always meant to be.

Affirm:

I am in control of how I show up.
I am in control of what I focus on.
I am in control of how I react.
I am in control of myself.

I hope this season of life provides you with tangible proof that you're on the right track. I hope you see that all your hard work is paying off. I hope your optimism is restored. I hope your faith is rewarded.

When was the last time you sat and gave yourself credit for how much you've grown and how far you've come? When was the last time you celebrated a relatively small win, just because?

When was the last time you said out loud, "I'm really really proud of myself"?

A gentle push:

Your perspective is relevant, and your ideas are worth exploring. Stop trying to evaluate their worth before giving them time and space to fully form.

There's a big difference between finding the silver lining in a terrible situation and forcing a dishonest, toxically "positive" perspective that prevents you from sitting with how you actually feel.

You deserved better than what happened to you—and you still do.

You shouldn't have to live with the consequences of somebody else's bad choices. You shouldn't have been left to carry feelings of resentment, paranoia, or worthlessness because they chose to violate your trust. You didn't need to experience life-altering trauma to become the person you are today.

You're allowed to be angry.
You're allowed to be sad.

You don't have to forgive.
You don't have to forget.

Burying your socially unacceptable emotions won't change the way that you feel.

Blaming yourself for other peoples' choices won't undo the harm they've done.

We're all experiencing life through the lens of our greatest hopes and deepest sorrows. There is no form of gaslighting, denial, or emotional suppression that can remove our experiences from our subconscious. There is no way around feeling.

You can't "fake it til you make it" through your own healing process. You deserve the real thing—and your genuine healing process will require time, intentionality, and effort.

Please, be patient with yourself—but be real with yourself, too.

You deserve relationships rooted in love, not envy. You deserve friends who want the best for you, even if that means you have to take space from each other. You deserve people who cheer for you wholeheartedly, not just because they think they'll benefit from being close to you.

6 ways to stop negative self-talk:

—Remind yourself how far you've come.
—Remember that feelings aren't facts.
—Accept that nobody's perfect.
—Celebrate your small victories.
—Stop comparing yourself to others.
—Give yourself the same
grace you give to others.

When you work for their applause, you're a prisoner to their opinions.

Who would you be if you never carried the burden of maintaining appearances? Who would you be if you never felt pressured to live up to other people's expectations? We'll never know—but it's not your fault.

The truth is: as human beings, we are biologically programmed to seek approval from other human beings. We're not at fault for caring what other people think—we're simply living into our needs. It's a natural, human behavior.

"I don't care what people think" sounds great, but it's not realistic. It might be more realistic to say: "I do care what people think. I accept this part of myself, but I will not seek approval at the expense of my values."

Forgive yourself for all of the moments when your human instinct to seek approval takes precedence over your beliefs, values, and needs.

Instead of blaming yourself, push yourself to be aware. Recognize the moments when your desire to seek approval is pulling you out of alignment or away from your purpose.

Sending love to everybody who is struggling to enjoy the life that they worked so hard to build. Sending love to everybody who can't shake the feeling that everything is going to fall apart. Sending love to everybody who's scared of losing it all.

It's never too late for you to give yourself the grace that you so desperately needed as a child. You have the power to break the cycle of perfectionism and shame that's been imposed upon your lineage.

When you love yourself, you listen to yourself. You trust your intuition. You honor your heart's desires. You remind yourself that your feelings are valid. You acknowledge every emotion that passes through your body.

Sometimes all you can really do is take life one day, one hour, one minute at a time. You can't change the past or predict the future, but you can make the most of this moment that's right in front of you, right now. Tap in.

Affirm:

I know myself. I am committed to learning myself more deeply. I hold myself accountable. My knowledge of self protects me from the negative projections of others.

Nobody has the "perfect" thing to say in every situation, but we all can speak from the heart. Don't let fear of being misunderstood be the reason that your true feelings remain bottled up forever. Give yourself a chance to be heard and trust that the people who want to understand you will put forth the effort necessary to make that a reality.

Late bloomers
still bloom.

I hit a low point at the age of 27.

There was no singular catastrophic event that pulled me down into that dark space—it was my life, and my interpretation of my life. It was the way I thought of myself. It was the way I spoke to myself.

It was everything.

I was reckoning with a deeper awareness of what I needed out of life, while realizing how far away I felt from that life.

I was neurodivergent and I didn't know it—but what I did know was that I was tired of being labeled as lazy, dumb, incompetent, or messy for my shortcomings.

I wanted to build deeper friendships but didn't know how—I had yet to heal from a lot of the trust issues that I picked from living life as a teenager with an intense desire for connection but a lack of discernment.

I had been out of school for too many years to have

the hopeful naïveté of my young twenties, and I was too far away from the more successful years of my career to see the light at the end of the tunnel.

I wish that 33-year-old Michell could go back in time and tell 27-year-old Michell that everything was going to be okay.

I wish I could tell him that it was okay to ask for help in imperfect ways. I wish he knew that it was safe to cry.

I wish he could give himself a chance to embrace life for the beautifully complicated mess that it always is, instead of waiting for the non-existent moment when everything felt "right."

I wish that I could tell him that he wasn't alone in what he was experiencing. I wish he could see that he would go on to alchemize all of his pain and find his purpose.

I can't go back in time, but the thing is: 33-year old Michell still needs to hear these things.

So I'll tell him, too.

I think you should give yourself more credit. Celebrate the way you've carried every burden life has placed on your shoulders. Be proud of the way you've pushed past every obstacle. You didn't ask for the hand you've been dealt, but you're making the most of it.

Protect your boundaries today so you don't have to burn bridges tomorrow.

Trust yourself.

Don't just say that you do. Act like it.

When you hit rock bottom and have no idea what's next, take a deep breath and remember that you're more than capable of handling anything that life throws at you.

Trust yourself.

Affirm:

I can adapt to any change that life throws my way. I can find the good in any situation. I surrender to the flow of life.

"It gets better" doesn't mean you should sit around and wait for things to get better. It means you should trust that things will get better while continuing to do your part.

Don't just keep the faith, act on your faith.

Abundance mentality in action:

Refusing to force anything—friendships, relationships, opportunities—because you understand that you'll find everything that's meant for you, in due time.

With every chapter comes more unlearning. More outgrowing. More deprogramming. Accept the changes as they come. Choose the freedom of fluidity over the fragility of rigidity.

Say it with me:

I will not dwell on mistakes
that I've already made.
I will not stress over outcomes
that I cannot control.
I will not carry burdens that
are not mine to bear.

Every chapter of your life has something to teach you—even the chapters that you wish you could skim through or skip over. As you turn the pages, give yourself time to read between the lines.

Honor your most difficult seasons. Accept your lowest moments. Release all forms of shame and guilt attached to your shortcomings. Practice radical acceptance of everything in this world that's out of your control. Love yourself, always, in all ways.

You're not the same person you were five years ago, so why carry yourself like you are? You can reinvent yourself as often as you need to. The people who are meant to stay in your life will be excited to adjust.

Affirm:

I trust myself. Deep down inside, I know what's best for me. I release self-doubt and make space for clarity. I acknowledge my fears, allow them to subside, and move forward.

“Nah. Bigger.”

—God

I don't know who needs to hear this, but it's ok to change your opinions as you learn. There's no shame in letting go of beliefs that no longer align with the person you've grown to be.

Please, take time to learn yourself. Take note of your weaknesses. Embrace your strengths. Confront your limiting beliefs. Understand your triggers. Be clear on who you are outside of other people's projections and assumptions.

No one can do this work for you, but every person you love will benefit from your commitment to building self-understanding.

A gentle reminder:

You will never hear another person's voice more than you hear your own. Be intentional about the way that you talk to yourself.

Scarcity mindset lies to us—it tells us that only one of us can make it. It makes us jealous of people we'd be better off supporting and learning from. If we're not careful, scarcity mindset will have us competing with each other for scraps when we could all be feasting at the same table.

Instead of being jealous of people who are more accomplished than you, let their existence serve as inspiration. Look at them as examples of what's possible. Let go of that scarcity mindset and walk confidently into the abundance that you deserve.

There is no perfect person. There is no perfect season. There is no perfect opportunity. There is only the present moment and what you choose to do with it. Don't miss out on the good that's within reach because you're waiting on the perfect that will never come.

We're all figuring things out as we go. We're all finding our way, and given that the world around us is constantly in motion, it's natural that we'll all feel disoriented from time to time.

When you feel lost, try to be kind to yourself. No, you don't have all the answers—none of us ever will. We're all bound to make mistakes and fall out of alignment with our values and goals.

If you're pursuing perfection, you're setting yourself up for permanent dissatisfaction. Instead, pursue resilience. Give yourself as many chances as you need to get back on track.

There's no such thing as a bad time for you to recommit to yourself.

Tap back into the daily habits that bring you peace. Reconnect with the parts of yourself that you've been hiding from. Make sure your inner dialogue is grounded in love. Give yourself the love that you deserve.

I hope this season of life breathes new energy into you. I hope the weight on your shoulders feels like less of a burden and more like an opportunity for growth. I hope you spend less time looking in your rearview and more time watching the road ahead. I hope you find joy.

Sending love to everybody who is trying to outrun the trauma of their past. Sending love to everybody who is trying to imagine a better future for themselves. Sending love to everybody who knows that they need to heal, but doesn't know where to start.

Heal so you can love more deeply. Heal so you can live more abundantly. Heal so you can express yourself more freely. Heal so you can see the light that has always been inside of you.

I hope this season of life is kind to you. I hope you experience moments that you'll never want to forget. I hope you can see the universe responding to your consistent effort and genuine intent.

Affirm:

I am growing into the most aligned version of myself. I am proud of the person I am becoming. All of my hard work is paying off.

There's nothing wrong with taking an unconventional path. There's nothing wrong with moving at your own pace. There's nothing wrong with choosing what's best for you, even if it's unpopular. *Honor your journey, not other peoples' opinions.*

The art of clearing your mind so that you can listen to your heart

My fellow overthinkers:

I know this is easier said than done, but please stop beating yourself up for the mistakes that you've already made. Please understand that holding onto guilt won't change the past.

You can forgive yourself, and learn from your mistakes at the same time. Instead of punishing yourself for honest mistakes, empower yourself to do better in the future.

Less "what if i'm not
good enough?"

More "what if i'm better
than i think i am?"

Sending love to everybody who always feels weird—like they never fit in but they don't stand out, either. Sending love to everybody who has too many acquaintances but not enough friends. Sending love to everybody who is still searching for somewhere that feels like home.

Plot twist: you're not lost—you finally have a chance to explore yourself without being tied to a specific outcome.

Give yourself permission to change the story that you tell yourself about yourself. You're not defined by your failures, or the hurtful things that people say about you, or the pictures that anxiety paints inside your head.

You can define yourself, for yourself.

Don't let a hypothetical future situation detract from the happiness that you can be experiencing right now. When you feel yourself slipping into a dark space, please try to remember that you can be prepared for the worst without expecting the worst. Remember that you can prioritize your joy today and solve whatever problems may emerge tomorrow.

The life that you've been dreaming about is possible—you just have to believe in your ability to create it. Keep the promises that you made to yourself. Remind yourself what you're working towards. Use every tool at your disposal. Give yourself a chance. When you don't feel good enough, just focus on taking one small step forward, and let that be enough for the day.

Try to be kind to yourself today.

If anxiety creeps in, remember that feelings aren't facts. If imposter syndrome crashes the party, remember that you can do it scared. If perfectionism pulls up, remember that "done" is better than "perfect."

Reframe the narrative: resting isn't lazy, it's necessary.

Affirm:

I am healing. I am whole. I deserve to be happy. I know that the pain I feel in my heart is temporary. I am ready to acknowledge and release all of the guilt and shame that I've been carrying inside of me so that I can make space for the life that I deserve.

Shout out to everybody who's frustrated, exhausted, or scared, but still doing the best they can with what they have.

No more watering yourself down to make them more comfortable. No more silencing yourself to protect their egos.

I don't know who needs to hear this, but meet yourself where you're at. Stop holding yourself to standards that you're not equipped to maintain. Don't let your perception of somebody else's way of being make you rush your process.

The art of rediscovering yourself over, and over, and over again.

Shout out to everyone choosing faith over fear, even when the odds are stacked against them. Even when they don't know how much longer they can hold on. Even when they have no idea what's next.

Affirm:

I know that all of my problems are temporary. I know that better days are coming. I know all things are working out for the greater good.

Building something from the ground up is exhausting—but if you build it right, it's yours forever, and the lessons that you learn from putting in hour after hour are worth their weight in gold.

I hope you know that you don't have to apologize for the way that your boundaries inconvenience other people. It is not your job to accommodate other people at your own expense.

"It's not that deep," until it is. Sometimes your emotions are too much to process all at once. Sometimes you need space to push back against your inner people-pleaser so that you can be honest with yourself about how you really feel. Sometimes you have to sit with your feelings before you can work through them—not because you're weak or inadequate, but because you're a living, breathing human being.

Please, be gentle with yourself. You're still learning. You're still growing. You're doing the best you can. Love yourself through every peak, valley, and plateau on your journey.

If keeping up with your daily habits and obligations feels more like a burden than an opportunity, maybe it's time to flip the script. Maybe it's time to remind yourself of exactly what you're working towards.

Obligations are heavy but excitement is invigorating.

It's easier to stay committed when you're clear on what you'll get in return for your dedication. Ask yourself, "how will these habits make me a better person over time? What will this better version of myself be able to accomplish, attract, and manifest? What kind of person am I becoming?"

Give yourself something to look forward to. Think about the personal transformation that you are manifesting, day by day. Think about how accomplished you'll feel in six months, or six years, as the compound effects of your daily habits continue to resonate throughout every facet of your life.

Don't be afraid to fail in public.

People who are doing the work will be too busy to judge you for your shortcomings. People who are spectating wish they had the courage to jump into the arena. Your growth is more important than your pride.

Sometimes all you can really do is take life one day, hour, or minute at a time. You can't change the past or predict the future, but you can make the most of the moment that's right in front of you, right now.

Congratulate yourself for your silent, hard-fought, inner victories. Just because no one else knows about it and few can relate to it doesn't mean it's not worth celebrating.

Self-care should be a daily practice, not an emergency procedure.

They can copy your aesthetic, bite your style, and mimic your moves, but they'll never overtake the original. They'll never be you. You're one of one, always and forever—operate accordingly.

Commitments rooted in self-love:

I promise to never give up on myself.
I promise to speak up for myself.
I promise to protect my energy.
I promise to give myself grace.
I promise to honor my calling.
I promise to forgive myself.

The art of knowing
when to pivot,
when to pause, and
when to persist.

Affirm:

I'm on the right track. I'm making my future self proud. My choices are in alignment with the path I have chosen. I am growing into a more healed version of myself.

Sending love to everybody fighting silent battles. Sending love to everybody who is grieving unmet expectations. Sending love to everybody who wants to ask for help but doesn't know where to begin.

Plot twist:
you're more powerful
than you think you
are, you just have to
move accordingly.

Free yourself from unrealistic expectations.
Free yourself from the need to be impressive.
Free yourself from goals motivated by ego and pride.

Focus on your ability to be impactful, instead.

Sometimes you have to choose the commitments you've made to yourself over the excuses that make you feel better in the moment. Sometimes you have to remember that you're better than the narrative that your anxiety is creating in your head.

Sometimes you have to do it scared.

We are all doing our best.
We are all navigating difficult decisions.
We are all beautifully complicated human beings.

When you think about the people in your life, don't just think about the parts of their lives that you're aware of—remember that they are bearing the weight of invisible burdens, just like you. Remember that they are healing from unspoken trauma, just like you.

Set your boundaries and protect your peace but try not to take things personally, because there is so much going on beneath the surface that you will never understand.

I know that you're busy.
I know that life is crazy.

I know, there's always a new problem to solve and a next step to take.

Life isn't slowing down any time soon, and it's hard to make space for introspection—but please, don't spend your whole life in such a hurry that you can't even take a moment to celebrate yourself and how far you've come.

Don't let your gratitude journal collect dust forever. Don't forget to congratulate yourself for making it this far.

I love those moments when I realize that I did exactly what I said I was going to do. I love conversations with myself that help me to see that my dedication is paying off. I love proving myself right.

Every minute you spend trying to prove yourself to other people is a minute that could be spent appreciating the person you've already worked so hard to become.

Choose yourself.

It's a beautiful day
to stop dwelling on the
past, stop worrying about
the future, and start
living in the present.

This world will bruise you. And sometimes, it feels like you never get enough time to heal before another wound is inflicted.

We're all walking around with smiles on our faces and scars over our hearts.

We're all faced with the seemingly impossible task of getting back on our feet, while knowing that this won't be the last time that life knocks us down to the ground.

But we deserve to experience more sunshine in this life, and the happiness that we deserve is on the other side of our willingness to keep stepping out of the darkness to reassemble the parts of us, and each other, that have been broken.

Affirm:

I show up for myself every day.
I give myself the consistency that
I deserve. I'm excited to see how
my habits shape my future.

If only you knew how powerful you'd become once you stopped waiting for other people to confirm what you already know is true.

Sending love to everybody who is trying to be patient with themselves while living in a world driven by a false sense of urgency. Sending love to everybody who is trying to live in the moment while worrying about what happens when they run out of time.

The best writers in the world need editors.
Elite athletes need skill coaches.
Therapists need therapy.

Needing help doesn't mean you're bad at what you do—it means you're smart enough to know that you'll never be the best version of yourself if you try to do everything alone.

A gentle reminder:

Resist the urge to obsessively compare your life journey—which you know intimately well, to other people's highlight reels—which you see in passing.

Happiness takes work.
Success takes work.
Love takes work.

Life takes work.

Get clear on the type of life that you feel is worth working towards, because that life is waiting for you to build it.

Affirm:

I handle setbacks with grace, poise, and patience. I give myself the time that I need, acknowledge every emotion that I feel, and continue forward. I know that I am doing the best I can with what I have.

Your value as a human being doesn't decrease when you can't show up as your best self. You're still the same powerful, capable person when you don't do any work at all. Instead of constantly trying to prove your worth, understand that you're inherently valuable. Start there.

Staying committed to healthy daily habits is like writing a series of love letters to your future self.

Focus on what you can control.

Why? Because when you do, you ground yourself in the present. You pull yourself back into a more mindful space. You empower yourself to think constructively. You force yourself to stop ruminating. You take your power back.

**Who are you
when fear isn't holding
you hostage?**

The next time you're about to talk yourself out of shooting your shot, remember that there are less qualified people with more confidence who are winning, simply because they never stopped shooting.

You don't have to reject the compliments that people give you. You're allowed to accept the fact that people love, appreciate, and value your presence in their lives. You get to form your own opinions of yourself while appreciating the kind things that people say about you.

Contrary to popular belief, you don't have to bully yourself into being a better person. You can be proud of the person you are while working towards becoming the person you want to be.

You're allowed to love yourself as you grow.

Sending love to everybody who is fighting their way out of a cycle of overthinking, paralysis, and regret. Sending love to everybody who is ready to escape the prison of perfectionism.

This chapter of your life might feel more uncomfortable than you want it to, but the discomfort you've been avoiding might end up being the impetus for the growth that you've been hoping to manifest. This part of your life might be more of a hands-on project than a passive experience. You might have to ask yourself some difficult questions. You might have to let go of some situations that feel comfortable but stunt your growth. You might have to get your hands dirty.

You might have to remind yourself that the tests come *before* the breakthrough.

If you build it right, you only have to build it once—so be patient with yourself. Take things one step at a time. Stop trying to expedite your lifelong calling.

Affirm:

I know what I'm doing. I know where I'm going. I trust my instincts, even when they carry me outside of my comfort zone.

Shout out to everybody who knows they deserve more than what the world is giving them. Shout out to everybody who feels like their next breakthrough is long overdue. Shout out to everybody who is trying to remain patient.

**The art of knowing
when to speak,
when to listen, and
when to leave**

Sending love to everyone who wants to do better but can't find the energy to make the necessary changes. Sending love to everyone who wonders if their exhaustion is permanent. Sending love to everyone who's tired of feeling stuck.

Learn to let go
when it's time to let go,
not when you have
no other choice.

You did your best.

You made some mistakes, but you did your best. It might feel like you let people down, but you did your best. Things didn't turn out the way you had hoped, but you did your best.

You did your best.

Let these four words carry you through your low moments.

Remember that even when things don't go according to plan, you can still bring the lessons that you've learned into your next chapter. Peel back the layers of disappointment and frustration that are clouding your vision, so that you can experience the good things that are happening while you recover.

Affirm:

I am enough. Who I am is enough. What I do is enough. I accept myself unconditionally. I love myself unconditionally.

Stop judging your worth by the way people treat you.

Just because they're quick to discard you, doesn't mean you're disposable.

Just because they laugh at your goals, doesn't mean they're impossible.

Just because they don't clap, doesn't mean you shouldn't feel proud.

Shout out to everybody who's more exhausted than they can express but holding on as best as they can. Rest as much as possible, give yourself all of the grace, and remember that this season won't last forever.

Affirm:

I see beautiful experiences in my future. I see aligned opportunities right around the corner. I know better days are coming.

It's okay to take a break when you're feeling stagnant.

Sometimes you have to reset, reflect, and recover before you can push through.

It's natural to want support from the people around you, but their silence doesn't echo as loudly when you start clapping for yourself.

“Affirmations are meaningless.”

“Affirmations will change your life.”

Either of these statements could prove to be true, from your vantage point. You get to determine which one will apply to your life.

Affirmations are not magical spells, they’re tools—and like any hammer, screwdriver, or wrench, they only fulfill their desired purpose when handled with intention and with precision. Saying affirmations out loud without a desire to believe in what you’re telling yourself or act on what you believe is like tossing a hammer at a wall and hoping you hit a nail.

Before affirmations can play an active role in your personal transformation, you need to get clear about the parts of yourself that you already love, value, and appreciate—the parts of yourself that you will need to be reminded of during your moments of insecurity. Don't shy away from your strengths, focus on them.

Choose affirmations that remind you of how powerful you really are and read them to yourself, often. Allow these affirmations to serve as emotional anchors when negative thoughts are threatening to sweep away your confidence. Commit to showing up as the version of yourself that is in possession of the traits that you're affirming, and watch the affirmations that you repeat to yourself turn into self-fulfilling prophecies.

You won't feel stuck forever. You won't always have that sinking feeling in the pit of your stomach. And when your moment of clarity arrives, you'll be proud of how you persisted when you couldn't see any light at the end of the tunnel.

Let go of the belief
that people will stop
loving you if you speak
up for yourself.

I want to spend less time overthinking and more time living in the moment. Less time chasing the next big thing and more time appreciating what I already have. Less time worrying about what could go wrong and more time getting excited about the possibilities.

Shout out to everybody who's unlearning the old habits that won't serve them in their next chapter of life. Letting go is difficult, counterintuitive, and disorienting.

It's also worth it.

Your future self
is going to thank you
for not giving up.

Fatigue is real.
Overwhelm is real.
Exhaustion is real.

Don't feel guilty about needing breaks from a world that was never set up to protect your mental health in the first place.

Affirm:

I'm on the right track. My hard work is paying off. My sacrifices are worthwhile. I'm exactly where I need to be. The universe is working in my favor.

Please, don't settle for a surface-level connection when you know you're craving depth.

Please, don't rush into dysfunction when you deserve harmony.

Please, don't talk yourself into accepting the bare minimum.

Please, don't accept anything less than what you deserve.

Sending love to everyone who is tired of being tired. Sending love to everyone who feels like they're waiting for a "return to normal" that will never come. Sending love to everyone who is mourning the death of simpler times.

Access to you is a privilege. Your energy is finite and valuable. Your heart is worth protecting. Don't give away so many bits and pieces of yourself that you have nothing left to come home to.

A gentle push:

Consistency is powerful, but only when paired with mindfulness and intentionality. If you show up every day but operate carelessly, you're going to get very good at executing below your potential. Try to show up as the version of yourself that you want to be, every day—you'll be amazed at the results.

Shout out to everybody who is pushing through fear because they know a better life is waiting for them on the other side.

A personal goal I'm working towards:

I want to get better at letting go—of grudges, of resentment, of expired goals, of outdated beliefs, of everything that is getting in the way of my healing and my happiness.

A gentle reminder:

Expecting the worst won't protect you
from disappointment—it will only
detract from the joy that you could
be experiencing in the present.

Give yourself as many chances as you need to get it right. Don't keep score. Don't let guilt hold you hostage. Just keep learning, and keep going.

Do you ever just sit and think about who you're becoming and say to yourself, "wow, God snapped"?

You don't need to rush. Take your power back by choosing the pace that best suits the season of life that you're in.

Instead of proving them wrong, focus on proving yourself right. Pursue your own definition of success and discover true fulfillment.

As a kid, I fantasized about fame.

As a younger adult, I fantasized about wealth.

Now, I fantasize about a life of ease.

I want a life where my worth is not tied to my productivity, I get the rest my body needs, and I don't have to sacrifice time with loved ones to survive.

Shout out to everybody who's figuring out how to respond when their boundaries get tested. Shout out to everybody finding the balance between speaking their peace and keeping the peace. Shout out to everybody navigating complex relationships with people they love.

Just because you haven't experienced the life that you deserve doesn't mean that you never will. Don't let this world rob you of your imagination. New possibilities are waiting for you on the other side of your willingness to see them for what they are.

Keep going, because the best is yet to come.

Keep going, because you're stronger than you think you are.

Keep going, because every step forward brings you one step closer to your goals.

Keep going, because you deserve to see what happens when all of your hard work pays off.

I'm sorry they made you feel like you weren't good enough.

They poked holes in your accomplishments and found joy in your failures. They made you question yourself, over, and over, and over again. They positioned themselves as your judge and jury, when you really just wanted a partner in crime.

They said they were in your corner—but they never were, and when your relationship was no longer alluring or convenient, they showed their true colors. They said they loved you but pushed you away when you needed them the most.

You started to ask yourself, "Is it me? Is this my fault? Did I deserve to be treated this way? Should I have known better?"

But then you remembered that you don't have to judge your worth off of the way that other people treat you. You remembered that one relationship can never define you as a human being. You remembered that people's decision to repeatedly mistreat you is indicative of their character, not yours.

And now, you're here—understanding that you always have been and always will be worthy of being treated with care.

Healing.

A little more focused.
A little more thankful.
A little more consistent.
A little more thoughtful.

All of the little changes add up to make a huge difference.

You don't have to fix all of your problems at once. Give yourself the grace and patience that you deserve. Instead of rushing to meet imaginary deadlines, trust in your ability to persist. Trust in your ability to endure.

I'd rather slowly find
my groove than rush
into misalignment.

Sending love to everybody who feels like they have nothing to be thankful for. Sending love to everybody who wonders when things will get better. Sending love to everybody who is tired of waking up to a life that they never wanted.

The art of making space for what's to come

Celebrate your little victories. Be proud of the way you bounce back after an "off" day. Be proud of yourself for choosing consistency on the days when you don't even feel like showing up. Be proud of the moments of introspection that empower you to show up as the version of yourself that you want to be, instead of the version of yourself that you thought you had to be.

Affirm:

The best is yet to come. I have so many beautiful moments in my future. I will experience deeper levels of joy, love, and peace.

Are you humble,
or has trauma shown
you that it's safer to
hide parts of yourself?

Nobody talks about how hard it is to let go of what no longer serves you. We're human. We form attachments. We crave familiarity, even when it hurts us—but sometimes, we have to let go before we can see what we're making space for.

That's where faith steps in.
That's where God steps in.

Affirm:

I am resilient. I persist in the face of adversity. I always bounce back. I always find a way.

One thing about me:

I get tired, I get frustrated, I get burnt out, but eventually I get back to it, and I figure out what works.

You gain nothing from beating yourself up for mistakes that you've already made. Try to be kind to yourself when you fail. Look for opportunities for growth before you look for reasons to be upset with yourself. Don't punish yourself for failing, celebrate yourself for trying—and know that you can try again another day.

You don't have to prove them wrong—just prove yourself right.

Instead of ruminating on the people who question your abilities, focus on what you're working towards.

Hard boundaries to protect a soft heart.

I hope you're honest with yourself today. I hope you listen to yourself instead of deferring to popular opinion. I hope you trust your instincts, even when they carry you outside your comfort zone. I hope you understand that when you're honest with yourself, the healing begins.

Don't get so focused on what you want to be true that you can't see the good things that are happening as a result of the outcomes you were trying to avoid.

When you let go of the need to always be in control, you can better appreciate the reality that you're experiencing while continuing to work towards the reality that you want.

May time reveal to you that what felt like rejection was actually divine protection. May the perspective that comes in hindsight transform regret into relief.

Social media can be a distraction, or a tool, or a moodboard, or a resumé, or a catalyst, or an escape…

Don't let the options that are easiest to see make you lose sight of all the possibilities.

Maybe everything feels overwhelming and exhausting right now—not only because of what's happening around you but also because of what's happening inside of you. Maybe you're in the middle of your most profound transformation. Maybe you're being prepared for what's to come.

As you heal, I hope that you revisit the story that you tell yourself, and others, about who you are. I hope your story of self is rooted in self-acceptance. I hope you realize that you've always been doing the best you could with the level of understanding that you had at the time. I hope you remember that your story is far from over, and you're holding the pen.

Affirm:

I give myself permission to fail,
because perfection is a myth and
progression is not linear.

When you love yourself, you hold yourself accountable. You commit to not making the same mistake twice. You choose discomfort over complacency. You remind yourself that you deserve the best.

The art of loving yourself unconditionally

You're allowed to be proud of how far you've come.
Celebrating your growth doesn't make you arrogant.
Don't let people project their insecurities onto you.

Sending love to everyone who is carrying their burdens in silence. Sending love to everyone who wants to be heard but is afraid to speak. Sending love to everyone who's ever felt alone in a room full of people.

You ever realize that you've been holding onto something that no longer serves you only because of how hard you worked to get it?

You ever realize that you're in a toxic situation but struggle to believe that you can find anything better?

I have—I was the one who stayed, even when my heart told me to run away. I was the one who tried to fix things, even when my brain told me that this wasn't my fault.

I'm telling this story in the past tense because I can see things clearly now.

I overstayed my welcome in situations that no longer served me, and the hardships that I endured as a direct result of this choice forced me to reflect on the role that I played in my own suffering.

I stayed because I didn't want to be perceived as the "bad guy" for speaking my truth. I stayed because I was scared that I was wrong about my assessment of the situation. I stayed because I was scared to rock the boat.

So, I stayed—and this decision became more difficult to justify with every passing day. I was a volunteer at a charity organization, except instead of helping people in need, I was working to serve peoples' egos—until one day, when I woke up and decided that I was done.

This decision didn't come as the result of some sort of revelatory experience. I didn't run away in the midst of a mental breakdown. Nobody came to me with new information that spurred a decision. I decided that it was time to honor my values and my intuition over other peoples' opinions, and that was the only reason I needed to leave.

I hope you love yourself when you're up and when you're down. I hope you have empathy for every version of yourself that has ever existed. I hope you know that by virtue of your existence, you're worth celebrating.

No more dismissing your feelings.
No more ignoring your intuition.
No more avoiding your calling.

I want healthy growth for you—not motivated by shame, but by a desire to be the best version of yourself. In competition with no one except older versions of yourself. Healing. Loving. Free.

Trust the unfolding of your life. Many phases of your life will feel disorienting, but when the dust settles, you'll realize that you weren't being torn to pieces—you were expanding.

Sometimes the people whose approval you crave won't be the people who show up for you.

It's a gut-wrenching feeling—but it will pass. It'll be easier to let go of your hurt and disappointment when you focus on the people who remind you that you're worth showing up for.

Be kind to yourself today. Remember that the anxious voice in your head is just a voice. Create space for things that make you happy. Try to make sure your internal monologue is rooted in love. You deserve to be handled with care.

Ego says
"I can do it alone."

Wisdom says
"I don't have to."

How do you forgive yourself?

Lovingly. Gently. Patiently. By understanding that it's the only way to truly move forward. By giving yourself the same grace that you give to others.

Imagine how much your life would change if you gave yourself a chance to learn from failure instead of running away from discomfort and unfamiliarity. Imagine how much your life would change if you stopped waiting for outside confirmation and took your leap of faith.

Imagine how much your life would change if you decided to just go for it.

Sometimes "be patient" sounds great in theory, but rings hollow in the moment.

Sometimes life makes patience feel like a luxury that we can't afford to buy into.

A lot of us are impatient because it feels like we never have enough time in the day. A lot of us are impatient because we're conditioned to thrive on the false sense of urgency that society has imposed on us. A lot of us are impatient because we know that nobody is coming to save us if our lives take a turn for the worse.

It's easy for the most privileged among us to preach patience from their ivory towers, unaware of how it feels to navigate life without a safety net.

How do we remain patient when we know how unforgiving this world can be?

We can start by understanding our impatience for what it is—a feeling, driven by our perception of urgency, which may or may not be rooted in reality. Then, we remind ourselves that while our feelings are signals, they're not necessarily facts.

You can think of the impatient voice in your head as a friend who loves you and wants the best for you, but sometimes needs you to help them see the bigger picture. As the CEO of your life, you understand that while there is truth to what the impatient voice is saying, it's your job to listen to that voice with the proper context and framing so that you can apply their insights to your life.

When the impatient voice in your head tells you that you can't afford to take any breaks, remember that rest is essential for productivity.

When the impatient voice in your head tells you that you're falling behind, remember that comparisons don't matter when you're focused on fulfilling your unique, divine purpose.

When the impatient voice in your head tells you that you're running out of time, take your power back by finding ways to make the best use of the time you have.

A gentle reminder:

You don't have to be the "bigger person." You don't have to accept insincere apologies. You don't have to tolerate relationships that drain you. You don't have to show up for people who have no interest in showing up for you.

We are not machines.

We need rest. We need time. We need space. We need laughter. We need love. And perhaps most importantly, we need each other.

We didn't plan to become closed off to the world, but a lot of us were taught that it's safer to go through difficult seasons alone than to risk being vulnerable with the wrong people.

We learned this lesson the hard way—we asked for help, only to be judged and ridiculed. We poured into people who never truly appreciated us. We didn't just stumble, we fell flat on our faces—because there was no shoulder left to lean on.

We looked around for our support system and saw an empty room.

And as much as I don't want to hold onto this part of my story, how could I ever forget how it felt to cry out for help and hear nothing but the echo of my own voice?

Healing is not for the faint of heart. It doesn't happen on autopilot. It is a difficult, frightening process. Some days, you feel light. You realize that even though you're not the same person you were before the trauma, you're starting to navigate your triggers with a bit more ease and fluidity. Some days, you even feel excited to open back up and let people in.

Other days, you feel the weight of every burden that you've ever carried bearing down on your shoulders and your spirit. Vulnerability feels like a weakness. New friends feel like a liability. As you remember your darkest days, when you promised yourself that nobody would ever be able to hurt you like this again, your self-imposed isolation feels like a necessary form of protection against the unknown.

You wake up one day and decide that healing can wait, because today is about survival. You feel like it's better to be numb than to risk falling off of another emotional cliff. You decide to run from your feelings for another day, because it's the only way we know how to keep moving forward. You decide that you're better off pretending that everything is ok, even when it's not.

And while this is not the closing scene of your story, it's a valid chapter that can't be glossed over. You can't snap our fingers and become the person you were before the trauma. You can't pretend to be okay until you are okay. Band-aids peel off far too easily—you need the real thing.

You need time, space, and grace to walk the path towards restoration and uncompromising self-acceptance. Healing isn't a destination, it's a lifelong process—and I think we'll all be better off acknowledging how hard it really is, while choosing to believe that it's worth the effort.

Say it with me:

I can be proud of myself and want more
for myself at the same damn time.

Maybe you're doing better than you think you are. Maybe it's time to stop questioning every move you make. Maybe you should trust your process. Maybe you should trust yourself in full.

I love those moments when I realize that I'm handling a situation better than an older version of myself would have been able to. I love conversations with myself when I realize that the self-work has been working. I love realizing that I've grown.

Please try to be kind to yourself, even when you fail. You can be the soft landing space that you need when you stumble and fall.

You ever wish that life wasn't so complicated? You ever wish you didn't have to make so many decisions? You ever find yourself looking for an adult to tell you what to do—until you remember that you are the adult?

These thoughts occupy my mind more frequently than I'd like to admit. For years, I fed into a vicious cycle of nostalgia and regret, in which I would reminisce about the relative simplicity of my past to the point that I could no longer see the possibilities of the present moment.

When I was working part-time and finishing college, I would frequently reminisce on all the fun I had in high school.

When I graduated from college and started working full-time, I found myself craving the simplicity of undergraduate life.

When I got married, I would sometimes reflect on how much simpler life was when I was single, working, and living on my own.

When I became a father, I realized that I had been taking for granted the freedom that comes with being an adult with disposable income and no kids.

I spent years of my life craving a level of simplicity that I could never recognize in the present, but would always appreciate in hindsight. I wanted life to be black and white, but life forced me to reckon with every shade of gray that has ever existed. I wanted the "right" answer to feel obvious and evident, but every chapter was a "choose your own adventure" mission. I wanted what I had already experienced, but only after it was already gone.

Wash.
Rinse.
Repeat.

When I was able to see this cycle of self-sabotage for what it was, I decided that it was time to opt out. My decision prompted me to think about how the cycle started in the first place. I had to ask myself: "what is it about hindsight that makes these seasons so much easier to appreciate?"

Here's where I landed.

It's easier for us to appreciate life in hindsight because we can look back and see what actually mattered, and what was a distraction. We can still remember how we felt, but it's easier for us to separate our emotions from the situation. The bittersweet truth is that we often appreciate the good times when they're already gone—but we can break this cycle by choosing to be present in each moment, with gratitude.

Affirm:

I see beautiful experiences in my future. I see aligned opportunities right around the corner. I know better days are coming.

"Playing it safe" won't protect you from a dangerous world.

You might as well go after what you really want.

The most powerful version of yourself is waiting for you on the other side of fear.

Please try to be patient with yourself—not just in public when people ask how you're doing—but also in private, when the voice in your head tells you to quit, and imposter syndrome tells you that you're not up to the task, and anxiety tells you that you're too late to make a difference.

Ground yourself by focusing on one step at a time. Instead of worrying about how much time you have left, trust in your ability to adapt and endure. You'll find your way. You'll figure things out. But first, you have to trust yourself.

You have to be ok with losing people along the way. It's going to happen, whether you accept it or not. Trying to hold onto dead connections is only going to slow your progress and delay your healing. Let go.

At some point you have to be real with yourself about the gap between the life you want to live and the life that your daily habits are leading you towards.

You don't have to be perfect, just be committed. Be passionate. Be dedicated. Be sincere. Be focused. Be authentic. Be yourself.

It's a beautiful day to write down all the things that you love about yourself. Be your own biggest cheerleader. Celebrate yourself. Pour into yourself so that you can pour into others. It starts with you.

You're overthinking because you really care—you don't want to fail. You don't want to let people down—but no amount of planning, worrying, or over-analyzing can give you control over what happens next.

Breathe.

Loosen your grip.

Experience life as it comes.

Affirm:

I am proud of myself. I love every part of who I am. I am doing the best I can with what I have.

You deserve friends who will not only accommodate your growth, but celebrate it.

The thing is, this world won't just give us what we deserve because we have our hands out—oftentimes, we have to be intentional about creating the life that we need. We have to figure out how to respond when our reality isn't measuring up to our expectations, and to understand the role that we play in the dysfunctional relationships that we experience.

Sometimes the people we love will struggle to make space for our growth—not due to something that we've done wrong, or due to their malicious intent, but because when people change, the dynamics of their relationships change, too.

Sometimes, we are both well-meaning and self-absorbed, to the point that we become so fixated on our goals that we stop showing up as the friends that our people need. It's true that growth is uncomfortable, but not just for you—your growth may also feel uncomfortable to people who are used to having access to a particular version of you that no longer exists.

As you grow, you will inevitably lose people along the way. It's not always your fault—and it's not necessarily their fault, either. We all need to be honest with ourselves about how the people in our lives make us feel, release relationships that hinder our growth, and make way for those we love to grow too—even if that means saying goodbye.

Please, be patient with yourself.

You don't have to make everything happen at once—just keep fanning the flames and adding fuel to the fire. A slow burn can grow into a roaring flame over time.

A gentle reminder:

You're only the main character in one story—your own. We are all handling our own problems, insecurities, and trauma as best as we can. Try to be kind. Try not to take things personally. Try to be a reflection of the love and empathy that you hope to receive.

Somebody lied to you.

They told you that success happens overnight. They told you it was a "matter of time." They told you that consistency was enough, and skipped over the part about the intentionality that's supposed to come along with it. They made you feel like you were already doing everything right, and that the world just had to catch up.

They fed you a myth—and for a while, you bought into it, because it felt good. And feeling good was enough to get you started. But then you got to a point in your journey where the myth you had bought into started to lose its allure. You began to question the beliefs that had carried you through so many seasons.

For a moment in time, you lost faith in the process you had chosen—and as a result, you lost faith in yourself. You started to question all of the choices you made that led you to this point. You tried to run from a sudden, sinking feeling that all of your hard work had brought you to the wrong destination.

Then, one day, you stopped running.
You didn't change directions.
You didn't retrace your path.

You just sat with yourself—and in that stillness, you found yourself again.

Your eyes opened wider than ever before, and you realized that you had spent all of those years blaming everybody, every situation, and every thing except for the one factor that you can control—yourself.

You looked in the mirror, and, for the first time in a long time, you saw yourself, absent of the facades and unreasonable expectations and misplaced arrogance.

You saw yourself.

And in that moment, you saw a truth that you could never unsee. You saw that you had been traveling a path that no longer served you—a path that kept you in your comfort zone, away from discomfort and disconnected from reality. For the first time, you realized that all of the discomfort you had been running away from was meant to be faced, not avoided.

As you sat with this truth, your first thought was to blame yourself. How did you end up so off course? How could you spend so much time traveling a path that ultimately didn't serve you?

That's when it hit you: You *had* to travel all this

way so that you could see things from this vantage point. Your willingness to put one foot in the other, even when you didn't have all of the answers, is the only reason you realized that it was time to change course. Your journey thus far wasn't a mistake, it was necessary preparation for the next chapter.

As that revelation settled into your spirit, you knew exactly what to do next.

You took a deep breath, exhaled, and took your next step forward.

Instead of thinking of discomfort as an inconvenience, think of it as an opportunity to leave behind counterproductive habits and embrace new ways of thinking and being.

When we push through discomfort, we grow. We gain confidence. We discover new parts of ourselves. We learn to trust ourselves in different situations and realize that we're more capable than we previously imagined.

Growth will not always be a comfortable process. It shouldn't be. It's supposed to push you. It's meant to stretch you. It's designed to pull you outside of your self-imposed beliefs and limitations.

It's draining in the moment, but worthwhile in the end.

Forgive yourself for every moment you lost faith in yourself.

This might not be a day for you to go "above and beyond." This might not be a day for you to get ahead. This might be a day when you do what you must, and nothing more. This might be a day for you to take a breath.

A lot of us have been conditioned to just be thankful that we got in the room, when in reality, we're more than powerful enough to change the conversation at the table.

Less "what if everything falls apart?"

More "what if everything turns out better than I can even imagine?"

I hope that you're kind to yourself today. I hope you give yourself grace. I hope you think of yourself as a beautiful work in progress. I hope you give yourself credit for every step forward. I hope you remember how far you've come.

Sometimes your intuition is the only evidence you need. Sometimes you can sense that better days are around the corner. Sometimes you don't need anyone else to contribute to a two-way conversation between you and God.

When you know that your breakthrough season is on the way, *you* know. That knowing is enough. Don't question your feelings—receive them and allow them to fuel your continued ascension. Allow your faith to sharpen your focus and fuel your fire. Trust your gut. Believe.

Sometimes your need to have the last word is the ball and chain that tethers you to the ground, when there are entire universes of perspective and wisdom waiting to teach you new things as soon as you're willing to listen.

When you let go of the need to be right, you free yourself. As you release the shame associated with being wrong, you gain access to deeper levels of knowledge, human connection, and peace.

Be honest with yourself and others when you realize that you're wrong. Embrace the learning opportunity that comes with knowing what you didn't know.

Plot twist: you didn't miss an opportunity, you dodged a bullet.

Your hard work is gonna pay off.
Your persistence is gonna pay off.
Your patience is gonna pay off.

The next time you realize you're being too hard on yourself, think about all of the beautifully imperfect people that you love. You accept them as they are. You're thankful for them. You love them—flaws and all. You deserve that kind of love. Start giving it to yourself.

How much lighter will we feel when we forgive ourselves for all of the mistakes that we've already made?

I hope we all find out.

I hope we forgive ourselves for everything—full stop. I hope we remember that shame will never serve us. I hope we remember that perfection is impossible. I hope we speak to ourselves with the love and care that we deserve.

I hope we take every lesson learned and use it to better our collective and individual futures.

You can be proud of who you are right now—not just the person you have the potential to be, or the person they say you are, or the person you're working towards becoming.

Be proud of who you are in real life, right now, at this moment.

I hope you're gentle with yourself. I hope that you have empathy for every past version of yourself. I hope that when you tell your story, you give yourself credit for everything you had to overcome along the way.

Remember who you are.

Don't let fear make you forget what you're capable of. Don't let failure make you forget how powerful you are. Don't let other people's success stories make you forget how far you've come.

You can't avoid heavy emotions. You can't avoid seasons of darkness. We all have to wrestle with our demons. We all have to walk through fire—but when you choose to keep going, step by step, you will transform into the person capable of fulfilling your divine purpose.

Today is a new day. Set your intentions accordingly. Let go of shame. Let go of guilt. Focus on what matters. Focus on what you can control.

Your purpose is bigger than you, and it always has been. You have more power to change the world than you can imagine—but you'll fulfill your divine assignment in harmony with like-minded people, and in rhythm with God. You can't outwork divine timing. You can't rush an entire movement. Pace yourself.

Sending love to everyone who is trying to rediscover their voice after life made them believe that silence was safer.

You can still love the people you've outgrown.

Stop waiting for people who don't know what you've been through to validate how far you've come.

No more watering yourself down to make them more comfortable.

No more silencing yourself to protect their egos.

It's so hard to speak up for yourself as an adult when you grew up feeling like it was safer to bury your feelings and hide your uncomfortable truths. It's so hard to imagine that people will accept and embrace every part of who you are when you've been shrinking yourself for so long—but when you're willing to step outside of your comfort zone, rediscover your voice, and accept every part of yourself in full, your life starts to transform in beautiful ways that would otherwise never be possible.

Rediscovering yourself can be hard, time-consuming, frightening, and draining. Don't be afraid of the discomfort that comes with it. Don't be afraid to seek out the professional and community support that you need as you navigate this life-altering process. Don't be afraid to take the first step. Don't be afraid to start—because the rewards that come in the form of personal growth, happiness, and fulfillment are well worth the effort.

Say it with me:

I'm allowed to outgrow people.
I'm allowed to outgrow situations.
I'm allowed to outgrow versions of myself.

I know it's hard to forget the moments you're ashamed of, but please make sure you remember all of the times you made yourself proud, too.

You're so much more than your lowest moments.

Affirm:

I am thankful for my life.
I see abundance all around me.
I will take every opportunity to
reflect on the blessings that I've
worked so hard to manifest.

Self-awareness can be a double-edged sword.

You start to understand yourself more deeply, and all of a sudden clarity feels within reach. You realize that peace is more attainable than you thought—but with this deeper level of self-understanding comes a deeper understanding of the ways that you've been sabotaging your own interests.

Sometimes, ignorance really is bliss. Sometimes, it's easier to have a chip on your shoulder than it is to own up to your own shortcomings.

What do you do when you realize that you've been holding yourself back, all along? How do you believe in yourself when you know that you've been your own greatest enemy?

If you're highly self-aware but have low self-esteem, it's easy to fall into a space of excessive self-criticism. Every flaw that you find inside of yourself will feel like a threat to your identity that must be fixed immediately. Every past mistake feels like an indictment of your character.

If you're not careful, you'll start to pick yourself apart to the point that you question whether or not you're worth putting back together again.

When this happens, it's important to distinguish between how you feel about yourself in the moment and who you are at your core. Remind yourself that you've always done the best you could with what you had and what you knew.

Try to remember that your mistakes don't define you. Try to remember that you can simultaneously be your toughest critic and your own biggest fan. Try to remember that you are a beautiful work in progress, not an object to be fixed. Try to be intentional about the story that you tell yourself about yourself.

Please, give yourself grace. It doesn't matter how many mistakes you've made, or how far along in life you think you should be, or what other people expect from you. You're human, and humans make mistakes. Humans lose focus. Humans need grace. Allow yourself to be human.

Forgive yourself for the moments when you let your emotions get the best of you. You're human. You're meant to feel things. Sometimes feelings can be overpowering—but when the dust settles, emotions subside, and clarity returns, you can always come back home to yourself.

Do you ever think about how social media affects your self-image?

Every time we scroll, we see the parts of people's lives that they want us to see, while being painfully aware of so much more of what is happening in our own lives—the private and the public, the wins and the losses, the joy and the shame.

It's one thing to know that we shouldn't compare ourselves to others, but it's a whole different thing to not do so when we spend so much time seeing other peoples' highlight reels.

It's not easy to remain confident in yourself, but it's worth the effort. Don't try to build confidence around a belief that you're better than other people, or that you're immune to making mistakes, or that you don't have to work for what you want.

Instead, build confidence rooted in the understanding that the version of yourself that feels free to take risks, make mistakes, and learn through experience is the version of yourself that will find the most happiness and fulfillment.

You're already that person—now, put yourself in that position.

Instead of questioning yourself, lead with the understanding that you're more than capable of handling every opportunity, obstacle, and situation in your path. When you choose self-belief, you choose yourself.

Be your own biggest fan.

Love yourself through every season of life that you experience. Remember how far you've come. Pour into yourself, so that you can pour into others. Celebrate every step forward that you take. Stop looking for external validation and start trusting yourself. Keep learning. Keep growing. Keep going. Your time is coming.

Trust yourself today. Trust your body to tell you what it needs. Trust your mind to make the best judgment calls. Trust your spirit to tell you what's real.

If you want to avoid creative burnout, you have to stop trying to operate like a machine.

Take breaks, guilt-free. Slow down, guilt-free.

Try to balance passion for your craft with mindful awareness of your needs.

You know what's powerful?

Not being held captive by other people's opinions. Understanding that people's perception of you is less about you, and more about the way that they look at the world. Giving yourself to hear people's perspectives without accepting them as truth. Giving yourself the last word about the way that you live your life.

Look at you.
Out here.
Making it.

Despite being scared, despite not knowing where to go, despite wanting to quit everything, you continue to pick yourself back up and figure out how to keep moving forward.

Be proud of your commitment.
Be proud of your persistence.
Be proud of yourself.

They demand that you "prove your worth," as if they don't know how badly they need you. They want you to feel like they're your only option. They want you to be grateful for scraps, when you deserve abundance.

They discredit your dreams, because they never had the courage to chase after their own. They settle for manipulation because they don't know how to give you anything better.

Run.

Shout out to everybody who's going after everything they want, whether friends and family support them or not. Shout out to everybody who says "we gon' make it," and believes it. Shout out to everybody putting their faith into action.

**It's a beautiful day
to focus on finding solutions
instead of being consumed
by the problem at hand.**

The idea that you're scared to talk about today might be the idea that changes your life tomorrow.

The idea that you don't feel capable of executing today might be the idea that shows you how powerful you really are tomorrow.

The idea that you can't stop thinking about today might be the idea that you'll reference as a message directly from God tomorrow.

When you decide that your ideas are worth acting on, you free yourself from a lifetime of wondering "what if…?"

It's hard to see how far you've already come when you're immersed in the moment at hand, focused on the obstacles that are directly in front of you. Everyday life requires a level of focus, mindfulness, and attention to detail that can make the big picture feel out of reach.

During those moments when you're questioning everything, give yourself a chance to see the big picture again—sit back, take a deep breath, and give yourself a chance to remember how far you've already come. Taking a break won't always feel intuitive when you're sprinting toward the finish line—but life is a marathon, and awareness is more important than speed.

We're all beautifully imperfect human beings. We're all carrying some form of trauma that shapes the way that we view the world and ourselves. We can't always choose positivity in the moment, but we can commit to being more aware of our emotions.

When you feel yourself slipping into a space of excessive self-criticism, pause, take a few deep breaths, and think about what it would look like to be more kind to yourself in the moment.

How can you reframe your self-talk to focus on solutions instead of blaming yourself for things that have already happened? Reflection is productive. Introspection is productive. Being your own biggest bully is not.

It's never too late to admit you were wrong.
It's never too late to reconsider everything.
It's never too late to change directions.
It's never too late to rediscover yourself.

It's never too late to come back home.

Keep living. Keep healing. Keep pouring into yourself—not only for yourself, but also for the people who need the version of yourself that you're growing into. You are needed. You are necessary.

Plot twist:

You always had the juice, but now you're finally figuring out what to do with it.

Sometimes when I feel happy, fulfilled, or excited, I think about what it would be like to bottle up my emotions so that I could hold onto them forever. But when I feel angry, bitter, or resentful, I feel an urge to sweep my emotions under the rug and pretend that they don't exist.

The thing is, all of the emotions that we experience are equally valid—even the ones that go against our ideals or feel burdensome. It's not in our best interest to hold onto negative emotions forever, but it's important to take time to understand why we're feeling them before trying to release them.

Feelings are information. Take notes.

Instead of beating
yourself up for not
doing better back then,
celebrate the fact that
you know better now.

"That's how the world works" is not a valid excuse for someone who is trying to overstep your boundaries.

"That's how the world works" is not a valid excuse for someone who is trying to diminish the way that you feel.

"That's how the world works" is not a valid excuse for someone who is trying to take advantage of you.

Don't let people gaslight you into accepting repeated mistreatment because "that's how the world works."

When you let go of people who consistently mistreat and belittle you, you make space in your life for the people who will treat you with the love and care that you deserve.

A gentle push:

You deserve to feel excited about your future, but that's hard to do if you keep holding onto your past.

Control what you can today.

Show up for yourself and show up for your people. Protect your peace and protect your boundaries. Focus on what matters, not what's been sent to distract you.

Pausing before you respond is powerful because it gives you a chance to think about who you want to be in the moment, instead of letting your intrusive thoughts and gut reactions make that decision for you.

"You got brand new on us."

I sure did. I was drowning, and the people around me couldn't even hear me gasping for air. I realized that in my rush to make other people happy, I had left myself behind—and I was the only person in my life who wasn't benefitting from that unfortunate truth.

I let people walk all over me and told myself that I allowed it because I loved them.

I had to reset my boundaries. I had to rediscover myself. I had to get clear on who I am and what I stand for. As I found myself, I lost some people—people who were friends. People who called me "family" but treated me like a stranger when I needed them the most. People who may think of me as the villain in their story because they could never see the plot beyond their own perspective.

Some days, I feel sad about the people that I've lost. But then I think about all of the people who love me and continue to make space for every "new me" that will ever exist, and I realize that I'm exactly where I'm supposed to be.

It's a lot easier to imagine enforcing your boundaries in theory than it is to stop somebody you love from overstepping in real-time. We anticipate neatly packaged situations where a clear violation occurs and it's easy to say "no."

It's harder to anticipate situations where empathy for self is at odds with empathy for others. It's harder to account for moments when your brain tells you to protect yourself but your heart tells you to give without thinking.

We have to remember that boundaries actually help us to show up for the people we love in a way that is sustainable—and while holding true to your boundaries might feel uncomfortable at first, it's the only way that you'll be able to continue to show up for the people you love—including yourself.

A gentle reminder:

Better days are coming—even when you can't see the light at the end of the tunnel. When you feel overwhelmed or incapable, remember that feelings aren't facts. Ground yourself in the understanding that no season lasts forever. Keep going. Keep the faith.

You're unique. You're one in a billion. You're one of one. When you explore your passions and follow your heart, you create a blueprint that other people can try to replicate, but never overtake.

Remember that nobody can copy the original without consulting the blueprint. Keep following your path.

Reframe the narrative:

You're not lazy, you just need to find
a process that you believe in.

Growth isn't loud. It's not something that you can flaunt. It's not a spectacle—it's a process that radiates outward into every part of your being, and every part of your life.

As you continue to work on yourself, you'll grow into a version of yourself that is more aligned with the life that you want to live. As you find alignment, you'll start to attract elements of the life that you want for yourself.

And as you build the life that you've always wanted, you'll be able to savor every moment—because you'll know how hard you worked to make these moments possible.

Applause is fleeting, but you can be proud of yourself forever.

I hope you forgive yourself for everything. Full stop. I hope you remember that shame will never serve you. I hope you take every lesson learned and use it to better your future.

Life is better when you make space for what you love.

This world can rob you of every ounce of happiness that you possess—if you let it. You have to be intentional about giving yourself something to look forward to. You have to prioritize your joy.

Do you ever feel like your "one day I'll be ready" is more of a comforting lie than an empowering truth?

Do you ever feel like you're waiting for a "perfect moment" that might never come?

Do you ever feel like your overthinking gets in the way of your ability to seize opportunities as they come?

Maybe it's time to start asking yourself some questions you've never asked yourself before.

Ask yourself what it would take for you to be radically honest with yourself about how you've been getting in your own way.

Ask yourself what it would look like to take one step closer to the life that you want, today.

Ask yourself: "what if all of these imperfect moments are opportunities to let go of perfectionism and focus on becoming a better version of the beautiful human being that I already am?"

Your new life will cost you—it'll cost you your old life, the people you had hoped to bring with you, and the distractions that numbed the pain. But your new life will be worth the investment. It'll meet you outside your comfort zone, in a world that makes space for your growth.

Affirm:

I matter. I deserve to be happy and healthy.
I show up for myself by prioritizing
my wants, needs, and desires—and
when I show up for myself, I'm able
to show up for the people I love.

There are seasons to prioritize rest, there are seasons to prioritize healing, and there are seasons to prioritize hustle. I hope that you trust your internal rhythm and choose the sequence that works for you.

I didn't cry for at least five years—not because I never felt overwhelmed with sadness or overcome with joy, but because I didn't feel safe to acknowledge my emotions in real-time.

I was building some of the deepest, most accepting, and most honest relationships of my life, but a huge part of me was frozen in time—tethered to the season of my life when I cried out for help and heard nothing in response except for the echo of my own voice. I didn't make a conscious decision to stop crying, but I believe that my inability to release the shame, desperation, and sadness associated with that season of my life was related to my inability to have a physical release in the form of tears.

Numbness became my default—even as I experienced the emotional rollercoaster and gradual awakening of my mid-20s, I frequently felt as though I was having an out-of-body experience. I would observe my most intense emotions through a glass window, waiting for the smoke to clear so that I could be sure that nothing would explode when I re-entered the room. I could see myself, but I was scared to know myself.

Even as I became aware of the ways in which I was neglecting my own emotions, I didn't see a different way to function—I had been bottling up all of my resentment, sadness, frustration, anger, and fear for too many years, and I didn't know what would happen if I allowed all these emotions to resurface after they had been lying dormant for so long.

In September of 2021, I cried deeply for the first time in years. I was driving to physical therapy. Up until that moment, it had been a regular Tuesday morning—but all of a sudden, my eyes were too flooded for me to see straight and my hands were shaking to the point that I was scared that I might crash. All I could do was try to keep my eyes on the road and hope for the best.

I didn't even know why I was crying when the tears started to roll down my face. I still don't know exactly what led to that specific moment—but what I do know is that my body finally told me that it was safe to release. After a few minutes, my body stopped shuddering. My tears dried. My heart slowed back down. I released my death grip on the steering wheel.

The tears that poured down my face that day were composed of grief, anger, frustration, joy, and relief. They were the summation of unforgettable moments that, up until that point, had remained unprocessed: when I chose self-sabotage over self-liberation, when I exceeded my own expectation, when I decided to be vulnerable with the people I should have been protecting myself from, when I realized that what felt like "the end of the road" was just "the end of one chapter," when I looked in the mirror and saw a stranger.

I didn't know how much I had been numbing myself until I could feel everything again.

I had my life-altering moment of clarity in a Volkswagen Jetta on a Tuesday.

I had been in therapy for months. I had been healing for years. But during that car ride, things clicked—I had been carrying so much shame about certain parts of my life that I couldn't let go of the narrative that I was an inherently bad person for my past mistakes. I had been spinning my wheels trying to heal in solitude, when there were so many people in my life ready to pour into me and give me the support that I deserved. I had chosen to blame myself for the way that other people discarded me.

I had learned so much about myself and the world since I experienced suicidal ideations in 2012. I had grown from a boy into a man—but because I hadn't felt safe to re-examine my interpretation of what happened during that season with the deeper levels of understanding that I had gained, my shame remained static. I hadn't given myself a chance to re-examine the story that I was telling myself about myself.

I was trying to keep my eyes on the road but kept looking nervously in my rearview mirror, just in case my past decided to catch up to me and destroy everything that I had built in the present.

As I sat in the car that morning, I felt my relationship with shame started to shift in a way that I'll never forget. It was still a part of my psyche, but it no longer felt like a debilitating burden that I was meant to carry on my back for the rest of my life. For the first time that I can remember, I gave myself permission to imagine a life without shame. I gave myself permission to let the past be what it was. I gave myself permission to feel all the feels.

I was a few minutes late to physical therapy that day, but I still went. I still did my workout. I still drove home. I still hugged my wife and kissed my daughter. I still took care of my work deadlines for the day. Life went on. I moved forward. Being honest about my feelings didn't stop me in my tracks, it allowed me to operate with an open heart and mind.

For the first time in a long time, and possibly for the first time ever, I looked in the mirror and saw a familiar face. I was able to better understand myself, and as a result I was able to give myself more of what I needed. I was able to move on with my life.

Acknowledging my emotions in full has made me a better man. Letting go of what I had been holding in showed me that the world will not collapse when I take the time that I need to breathe, feel, and be present. I trust myself to be imperfect and unpolished. I trust myself to react and release. I trust myself to feel everything, because I know that I can cry and keep my eyes on the road at the same time.

Michell C. Clark is a writer, husband, and father from Virginia. Writing saved his life.

instagram.com/michellcclark

twitter.com/michellcclark

michellcclark.com

THOUGHT CATALOG Books

Thought Catalog Books is a publishing imprint of Thought Catalog, a digital magazine for thoughtful storytelling, and is owned and operated by The Thought & Expression Co. Inc., an independent media group based in the United States of America. Founded in 2010, we are committed to helping people become better communicators and listeners to engender a more exciting, attentive, and imaginative world. The Thought Catalog Books imprint connects Thought Catalog's digital-native roots with our love of traditional book publishing. The books we publish are designed as beloved art pieces. We publish work we love. Pioneering an author-first and holistic approach to book publishing, Thought Catalog Books has created numerous best-selling print books, audiobooks, and eBooks that are being translated in over 30 languages.

MORE FROM THOUGHT CATALOG BOOKS

All The Right Pieces
—Nakeia Homer

When You're Ready, This Is How You Heal
—Brianna Wiest

Everything You'll Ever Need
(You Can Find Within Yourself)
—Charlotte Freeman

Holding Space for the Sun
—Jamal Cadoura

You Will Feel Whole Again
—Parm K. C.

How Does It Feel?
—Andrew Kearns

THOUGHT
CATALOG
Books

THOUGHTCATALOG.COM